FEATURING

Introduction

JOHN VAN AITKEN

In this second edition we continue North in the streets and spaces of the city. From contested sites of demolition, to new imaginaries formulated in the studio and in domestic, digital and social space, the volume is testament to how the urban endures as one of photography's perennial objects of study. Like the first edition, North again reflects our belief in photography as a relevant tool for exploring our ever-changing world. Whether in Preston, Liverpool, Berlin or Guangzhou the image-makers create a conversation with contemporary life as they endeavour to make their surroundings legible. The diverse strategies and objectives of the graduates, postgraduates or alumni included here, evidence once more the student centred approach of photographic teaching at UCLan. We aim to highlight our commitment to everyday life as a meaningful arena for research and cultural production. From all of us who have made this second edition possible we hope you will enjoy the work.

Jonathan Purcell

THERE IS NO CITY. ONLY US.

Imagine the city. Only now. A moment. In this instance, a population of unfolding thoughts, emotions and drama. Moments. Each enriched and constructed in conjunction with the landscape that surrounds it. Politics of spaces. Territories. Alleyways, corners and doorways with an ever changing complexity of interaction, situation and emotion. The intricacies of human being. The collisions and the chaos, the euphoria and the despair, the subplots and the sideshows, the voyeurism and the voyages. In the city. The desperation to return and the longing to leave. Each life and each moment a glorious equal. There is no city. Only us.

In collaboration with Philip Michael Morris
Images by *Jonathan Purcell*
Words by *Phillip Michael Morris*

Kirsty watched the clock. The dawn forecourt was
deserted and she admired the light and the reflections.
There was beauty there that she knew others could not see.
At six Bryan would relieve her and continue selling fuel
to the taxis and the miscreants. She knew he would read
all the pornography. She finished her Snickers and leant
on her hand, nursing a stolen library copy of Murakami.
She glanced at the camera in the corner and made sure her
card reader was out of sight. She didn't rip everyone's card.
Only the people with poor footwear. They deserved it.

Dennis Kirkham backed his own horse with the same desperate luck. The hammer that struck his left metacarpal was well judged and deserved. A dramatic lieu of payment, but not his first. The Emergency Department's automatic doors hushed to a close behind him. His freshly bandaged hand ached as the silver splint flashed morning light. He slid the stolen greeting card in his blazer pocket and spotted a discarded half smoked cigarette at his feet. Opposite, Blackmeadow Hill pointed home past Flat 421a. If he walked quickly he would be home to make her breakfast. And wish her Happy Birthday.

William John Godwin did not wake, in spite of the crash
of the glassware in the street outside. An early morning
was seldom his to know. Snookered in a disheveled terrace
that was once his mother's, his cue lay at the bottom of the
stairs in its case. Blue chalk still marked his left hand. Just
another morning. He fought life with bitterness and old
excuses that convinced only himself. There was no future,
only now. Sleep without dreams. He dribbled and smeared
the chalk across his face as the bin lorry pulled away.
He was rubbish at snooker too.

Tired, Samuel Banner freewheeled down Union Street.
His bronchioles braced by freezing air that came in with
daggers from the ocean. He had three hours on the government
inspectors, before they would blame his failing school on him
and not the deprivation they ignored. Pedalling around the
hairpin, the splendour of civic buildings arched in a municipal
velodrome. He recollected his interview twenty years before
and stopped to admire St Bartholomew's School on the hill.
He wanted one last walk around on his own. He had already
decided that he was going to punch the lanky one in the face.

Erstwhile Ronald Jacobs hurled the orange peel into
the bushes as juice ran down his chin. His calloused
hands mimicked the cracked concrete service road on
the fringes of the industrial estate. The bus stop to his left
was similarly neglected. Across the road beyond the gorse
and the wooden fence, he saw the first floor light come on.
Her naked silhouette appearing at the bathroom window
unaware. He rolled the pips across his teeth as she stepped
out of view into the shower. You could set your watch
by her. His bus was not due for another fourteen minutes.

Arthur Visqueen was motionless and bent thirty degrees
forward in aisle five. He combed what remained of his hair
in the reflection of the freezer chests that ran the length
of the frozen food section. He saw a younger man in his
reflection and not the pallid nuisance that he had become.
He liked it here and often visited when he could not sleep.
Twenty-four hour retail brought function and company,
but his conversation never quite connected. It pushed people
away and most of the staff sought to avoid him. Everyone
except Carole Transom, who had a use for him.

Buzzed up fuzzy. Warm. Jacqueline blew a slow motion breath of nicotine and relief. Three lanes of heavy traffic began to clear from the rush hour inside her head. Escape from the power-pointed passive aggression. Her seat upon the nibbled concrete step, looking down upon the broken traffic lights and the converging crossroad commuters. She marveled at the simple democracy unfolding. A spectacle of coexistence and exchange. Shift workers and office angels extending courtesy and fairness. Harmony and civic symmetry. Waving each other home with their reflected smiles. New possibilities. A better place. And no red lights, only green ones.

Jonathan Purcell
is Photographer and lecturer, based between Berlin and Manchester. His practice is exploring the 'everyday' through photographing places whilst wandering and people by convening. *jonathanpurcell.eu*

Philip Michael Morris
writes novels and short stories. His work has appeared in the *New Welsh Review, Architectural Review* and published by *Capsica*. *@PhilipMMorris*

Graduates & Postgraduates

YEARS 2013–2016

ABIGAIL MOSS-COOMES

BECCA WOOD

CHARLES STANTON

DAVID LESTER

JASON ROSE

KIRSTY BURSTON

RYAN WAGSTAFF

SEING TA

TOM REES

ANDREA CARROLL

NICOLA BROPHY

Seeing and Unseeing the Urban Environment: A Critical and Contextual Response

GARY BRATCHFORD

Since the beginning of the 21st century, more than half of the world's population have been living in cities. Thus, for the majority of us, what we see is, first and foremost, shaped or informed by our now largely urban, everyday experiences. This phenomenon is rapidly becoming a global action. A century ago, only two of every ten people worldwide were city dwellers, now the global majority is urban. While existing cities expand their boundaries, places such as China, which became a majority urban nation in 2011, plan to move another 250 million people to its current and developing city-spaces (Mirzoeff, 2015). To cope with this state orchestrated migration, China, as well as other developing nations, including India, are building ready-made urban environments. In response, photographers have begun to critically and reflectively respond to the homogeneity of the 'new global city'. Acknowledging this identikit process, the German artist Michael Wolf's *Architecture of Density* presents the uniformity of cities like Hong Kong as utilitarian rather than modernist. Others, like Chinese artist Sze Tsung Leong or Israeli photographer Shai Kremer have taken a less direct approach. By examining their own national landscapes as spaces of erasure and development, each photographer subtly highlights how the demands of modernity are in conflict with the past, present and possibly the future site of their landscape.

Moreover, the urban is being replicated in spaces of abjection. On the edge of 'civility' and 'out of sight', temporary urban 'Do it Your Self' cities are popping up on boarder regions across Europe and the Middle East. From the 'Jungle' close to the Calais port terminal in northwest France to Za'atari in Jordan, the organic development of these spaces reflects some of the formalities of urban planning, including shops and streets, access ways, informal social spaces are clear demarcations between 'public' and 'private'. Thus, it is without refute that the urban landscape now plays a significant role in how we see and understand the world today. It is becoming the backdrop for acts of terrorism and insurgency as well as the setting for the mass movement of people, capital and commerce.

The urban is also the arena from which we learn to see and unsee. It is where we look for inspiration and where we often go if we want to challenge our sense of normalcy. It is often where the most progressive trends are pioneered and where conventions are contested. It is common knowledge that the world's leading fashion houses are located in New York, London, Paris and Tokyo. Moreover, these locations are young and networked; thus, it is no surprise that the inhabitants of these locations became the inspiration for Jason Rose's digital ethnography, *Contemporary Freaks*. A homage to 1980's New York underground disco club culture, Rose's work reflects the multifaceted youth subcultures of a global society that is personal, individual and referential all at the same time. The urban is also present in the work of Ryan Wagstaff's studio practice. Inspired by the Kowloon district in Hong Kong, Wagstaff uses studio props and lighting cubes as an allegory for the urban cityscape upon which his muse sits.

Other graduate students have pursued more forthright engagements with the urban landscape, foregrounding urban space as a site of on-going contestation. Akin to the images drawn from my on-going photographic survey in the inner-city suburbs of Manchester. The work of Kirsty Burston and Thomas Rees both use their camera to explore and question the social and cultural regeneration of two different areas within Liverpool (UK). A form of social-semiotics, each photographer frames the space of their enquiry in such a way that we are invited to read both the space and the objects within as signs, signs that cannot be divorced from the critical position of the photographer. In this regard, there is a clear intentionality to this type of photography yet the approach is also artistic. By contrast, some students have used photography as a tool for personal enquiry; such is the case of Nicola Brophy's *House of the Lord* series. Focusing on the members of the Church of Jesus Christ of Latter-day Saints in Preston, Brophy offers an intimate account of the congregation, its garb and community space. Brightly lit, the concurrent theme of natural light and religiosity is subtly present, the signs and icons of worship common with religious representations are replaced with a combination of tightly framed portraits and threshold spaces. Bringing the proximity of the lens, and thus the spectator close to the subject, Brophy's work offers a growing familiarity to the subjects and places that she has documented each time they are revisited. In equal measure is Becca Wood's touching and intimate series, *'Not an average 7 year old'*. In this instance, the urban is omnipresent as a setting but not the focus of the lens or the spectators gaze but rather, we are asked to consider life as sometimes difficult journey. This can also be said for the work of Seing Ta. The 're-housing' of culture is often part and parcel of living in a global society. The migration of people due to war, economics or even love is never straightforward. French historian, Pierre Nora's places of memory or *lieux de mémoire* plays a key role in identifying the importance of place and memory, a notion that is specifically telling in Ta's work. When we go somewhere new the issue of seeing becomes, if only temporally, a complicated process. How we see things, spaces, and objects are never fixed, nor is our approach. We often encounter new spaces, places and communities with caution. Ta's work bespeaks these cautionary tones in a way Woods, Burston and Rees do not. The sepia tones, memory like in their presentation are a telling sign of Ta's relationship with space, memory and his subject. In David Lester's piece, *'The Body and the Landscape'*, he actively removes the spectator away from the urban and into the countryside. While we are indeed an urban population, Lester turns his lens to the contours of our rural environment. Lester, like Woods and Brophy provide spaces for reflection on our health, spirituality and our bodies in their own personal, yet creative ways.

Continuing this creativity is the augmented reality of Charles Stanton's 'super structures'. Playing with the notion of reality and perception, Stanton builds new spaces from existing buildings. Shot on location then altered with Photoshop, Stanton's experimental black and white process of image composites questions the form, function and value of the original. Like Stanton, Andrea Carroll also uses black and white to striking effect. Focusing on the desolate Ukrainian city of Chernobyl, Carroll's work delineates a practice that can be read as both documentary and art photography. The series depicts the consequences of political and human upheaval consistent with aftermath photography and the expressive and timeless absence felt in a catastrophe site. For the work of Abigail Moss-Coomes we are presented with an image of two distinct human tragedies within one single frame. Closing the gap between time and space, Moss-Coomes use of the Farm Security Administration's 1937 Great Depression photographs and the recent refugee crisis are a comment on the reoccurring theme of human suffering and easily readable visual tropes that ensue. Coomes's creative post-production practice can be understood as part of a broader, on-going examination of photography's relationship with scenes of disaster, migration and the plight of those seeking refuge.

Dr Gary Bratchford
is a senior lecturer at UCLAN and Board Member: International Sociological Association Visual Sociology Working Group.
garybratchford.info

Abigail
Moss-Coomes

Becca Wood

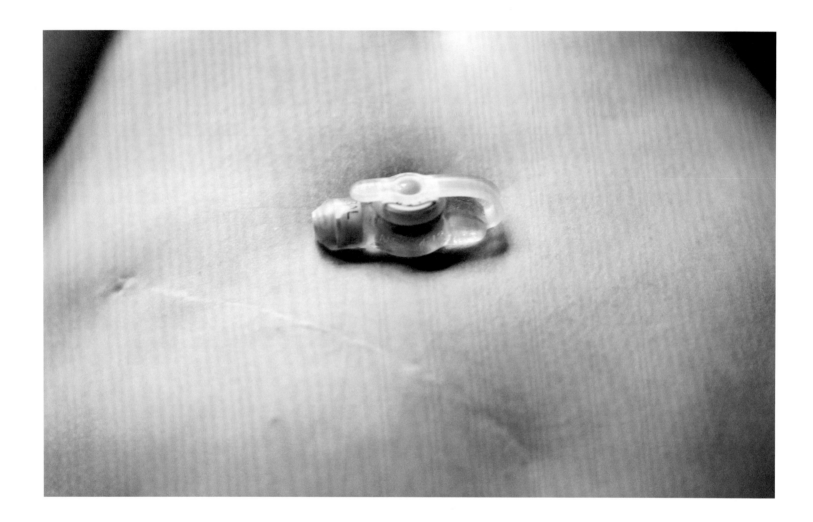

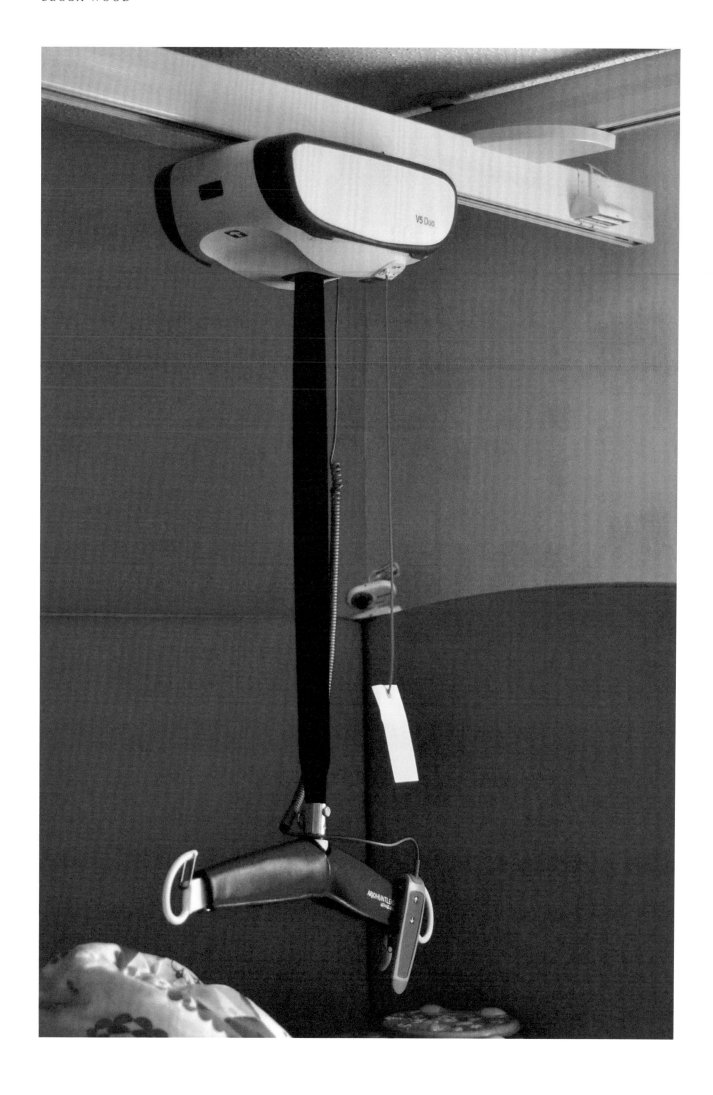

Charles Stanton

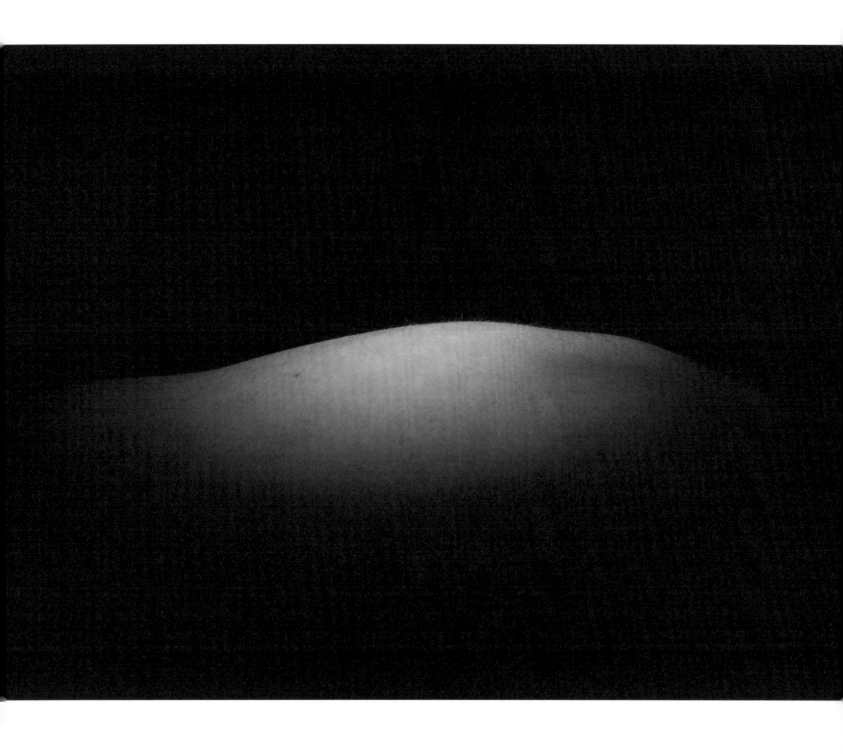

David Lester

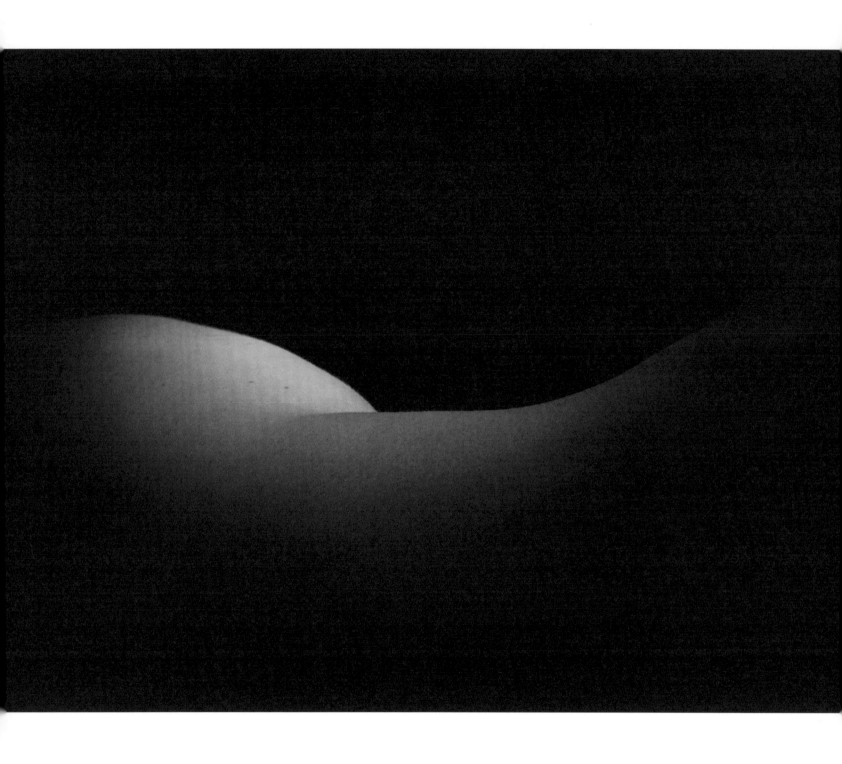

Jason Rose

Kirsty Burston

Ryan Wagstaff

Seing Ta

Tom Rees

Andrea Carroll

Nicola Brophy

Graduates

Abigail Moss-Coomes

(WEST SUSSEX, 1994)

bmosscoomes@yahoo.com
amosscoomesphotography.com

Becca Wood

(BURY, 1993)

rebecca_wood93@hotmail.com

Charles Stanton

(NOTTINGHAM, 1994)

charlie.stanton2@hotmail.co.uk

David Lester

(PRESTON, 1993)

davidpaullester@gmail.com
unwrittenphotography.co.uk

Jason Rose

(HACKNEY, 1994)

jasonrosephotography@gmail.com
jasonrosephotography.co.uk

Kirsty Burston

(LIVERPOOL, 1995)

kirsty.burston@gmail.com
kirstyburstonphotography.com

Ryan Wagstaff

(BOLTON, 1993)

ryan.wagstaff@outlook.com
ryanwagstaffphoto.com

Seing Ta

(GREATER MANCHESTER, 1994)

seingta15@hotmail.co.uk
seingta15.wixsite.com/seingtaphotography

Tom Rees

(LIVERPOOL, 1995)

tom@tomrees.co
tomrees.co

Postgraduates

Andrea Carroll

(LANCASHIRE, 1983)

andreacarrollphotography@aol.com
andreacarroll.co.uk

Nicola Brophy

(LANCASHIRE, 1986)

nicolalouisebrophy@gmail.com

Alumni

Lauren Jo Kelly

(MANCHESTER, 1990)

lozjokelly@hotmail.com
ljkphotography.co.uk

Kevin Crooks

(ST. HELENS, 1979)

contact@kevincrooks.co.uk
kevincrooks.co.uk

Lauren Jo Kelly

LIFE'S A DRAG

Images by *Lauren Jo Kelly*   Words by *Dale Lately*

The eyes ask the first question. Puddled in shadow, Bowie-streaked, and as bright as the screaming violet lipgloss. Then there's the long, feminine hand, bangled at the thin waist, perched over the top of a pair of stretchy dark tights. They're feminine legs, but the pose is masculine, muscular. Boy or girl? Man or woman? And why are we so obsessed with asking this question?

This is just one of the photos Lauren Jo Kelly, a young Manchester-based photography graduate, took of herself after deciding to check out the city's infamous drag clubs. But when some of the queens told her that she'd never understand their culture she did something nobody expected – she went home, dragged up, and came right back out to the club. Lauren took a gender reversal and reversed it again: she became a girl dressed up as a boy dressed up as a girl.

Dale Lately
writes on culture and communication and his work has appeared in the *Guardian*, *Slate*, *VICE* and *New Internationalist*.

The result was the *Life's a Drag* project, a set of photos which document her travels across the gender divide. It's not the first time that a photographer has "got among their subjects" of course; Kelly's work invites comparison with photographer Nikki S Lee, whose work documented New York street life – a gloved pensioner, a skater, a camera-snapping Asian tourist – until closer examination revealed that every photo was one of Lee herself. This is photography as chameleon disguise, dressing up taken to the level of total identity swap. Kelly and Lee become both performer and documenter, raising questions about the nature of both. But does their work also have a deeper significance?

"Men look at women. Women watch themselves being looked at" observed John Berger in *Ways of Seeing*. Women are forced to become observers of themselves, he points out, so the female self is divided down the middle – the woman "is almost continually accompanied by her own image of herself". She's both subject and object, both observer and observed.

This, perhaps, might be key to understanding Kelly's work. When Kelly embeds herself among Manchester's drag queens, a girl-as-boy-as-girl, she is performing both the "masculine" role of observer (photographer) at the same time as performing the "feminine" role (object). In this sense she can be slotted into a tradition of feminist performance art over the last few

decades, where artists such as Valie Export, Hannah Wilke or Carolee Schneemann manipulated their outward appearance in order to take control of how they were seen – in other words, employing the to-be-looked-at-ness of femininity as a tool to expose how they were being looked at. By dragging up, Kelly weaponizes her female role as object of the gaze. What could be more garishly and luridly attention-grabbing, after all, than drag? What could be more defiantly self-objectifying than the peacock world of queens? Kelly exulted in the attention; as she told *VICE* at the time: "People wanted to have their picture taken with me like I was some sort of celebrity."

This suggests another dimension on which we might appreciate these photos. We live in an age when self-documentation is stitched into the daily fabric of life, when the ongoing curation of our identity via digitally mediated images is second nature to an entire generation. We are all, so to speak, photographing ourselves now; Kelly's work serves as a commentary on this age of micro-celebrity. Photography, after all, is by its very nature an invasion of a space, a crossing of boundaries. In an age when digital media is quickly eroding old distinctions between audience and performer, making us all both spectators and participants at one and the same time, this kind of total immersion in the lives of others might be the only way to really feel at home.

John van Aitken

VISIT: XIANCUN URBAN
VILLAGE IN GUANGZHOU

With the rapid pace of urbanization in China since the early 1990's, the boundaries of large cities have expanded to encompass the ancient villages on their outskirts. The term urban village is used to describe these villages absorbed into Chinese cities and megacities such as Guangzhou. In the process of urban expansion villagers are persuaded to sell their agricultural lands, now prime real estate, to the municipal authorities for development projects. In return they receive compensation, are allowed to remain in urbanized enclaves and may be given permission to build or allocated new housing. The 800-year-old Xian village or Xiancun, which sits on the edge of Guangzhou's Tianhe district- an exclusive business zone and hub of the 2010 Asian Games- is typical of this situation. Many of the now landless Xiancun farmers took advantage of compensation schemes, built new houses or added levels to existing properties and started to earn a living by renting to migrant workers, in search of cheap accommodation. Xiancun has been at the centre of a dispute between villagers and corrupt officials who sold village lands illegally, a deal which was violently enforced by the police.

Yan arrives late, having been to the wrong underground exit. We are waiting at the top of exit C, having missed breakfast. The journalist is a little over 30, appears younger. He is pleasant, if slightly wary. This tour for foreign guests is performed out of duty and gratitude to Professor Zhang. Later when we have warmed more to each other, he jokes: "Professor Zhang owes me a meal for this!"

Yan drives us from the station where we met, to a small rank of parking spaces close to the building site of the East tower, which, at 530 metres on completion, will be the tallest building in Guangzhou. We cross the busy road via the underpass. On the other side, bear left towards a cutting in a section of wall and we slip into the urban village before we realize it. The wall is all that remains of the security cordon around the village but the identity checks and the violence, ended with the conviction for corruption of village officials who struck up deals to sell the village land to developers, against the wishes of the residents. Xiancun, whose origins go back 800 years, is in many ways typical of urban villages across China, at odds or in direct conflict with rapid urbanisation. Yan is old enough to remember the countryside that has now been consumed by the business district of Tianhe and metamorphosed into a forest of towers.

Yan strides, slightly ahead, but nevertheless making sure to accommodate our pace, slowed by equipment and curiosity. It gets better he keeps saying, when John makes to photograph anything. Our guide knows what a photographer has come to find in a place like this: moments of heightened drama; places where things connect, and places where disconnection is striking, extreme-scapes in which gleaming towers of glass and steel are indifferent to the wounded crumbling hovels beneath them. The photographer looks for human expressions of the drama too: people picking life through the remains of hope, hanging washing in war zones; a monk crouched by a lake that reflects only concrete; a child with the worlds weight in her eyes. And so on. These tropes.

Before we reach the monk and the lake we pass shops and stalls, sacks of rice, a sewing machine awaiting a seamstress, a man stripping the plastic outer layer from electrical cord. The passageways between buildings contract, reduced to narrow channels of grey silt etched by a trickle of effluent, impassable on foot, trapping rubbish. The houses get closer to each other, they are called 'holding hands' houses, Dr Zhang tells us later. Otherwise they are 'kissing houses'. We take a slight detour through the market. Once the villagers would have grown vegetables, kept livestock and fished in the Pearl River and all this produce would have been sold on the market. Now it has to be brought in from further afield, but still the market is busy. There are tables fringed with the kai lan or Chinese kale that we eat as often as we can get it-, which is practically every mealtime. One table is covered with twists of dusty, greying organic matter set out to dry. None of us know what this is.

Now we are going further into the area of the village where the demolitions have taken place. I tell Yan I keep thinking

Images by *John van Aitken*
Words by *Jane Brake*

Institute of Urban Dreaming
John van Aitken is the Course Leader
of the MA Photography at Uclan.
Jane Brake is a Senior Lecturer at
Manchester Metropolitan University.
Together they collaborate at the
Institute of Urban Dreaming.

Their work attempts to create
a conversation about housing,
social cleansing and the
consequential geographies caused
by contemporary accumulation
strategies. *iudblog.org*

about a film I have seen of a group of volunteers looking for survivors in a devastated section of Gaza. Yan, wordless, takes in what I have said. The devastation in Xiancun, however, is wreaked by the slow violence of bulldozers not the violence of bombs. Under our feet is grey clay-demolition dust mixed with water. The ubiquitous stripey polypropylene tarpaulins line the passageway and shield from view some of the rubble- keeping the light out too. The sound of a scooter approaches us with incremental volume and clarity, ominous with the potential for collision. Liquid drips on metal, out of sight, somewhere above our heads. Ping, pang. Pang, pong. Pang, pong. The scooter passes, followed by a man carrying a sack over his shoulder. They both turn right. My camera follows them along the increasingly narrow path, just too late. A shaft of light falls between the buildings, illuminating grey tones of wall and floor.

Yan is proposing to take us up onto the mound of rubble that forms a high level concourse between the hollowed out buildings. It is a steep climb up several metres of loose looking rubble. Yan is encouraging or rather threatening that I will regret it, if I don't go. I know this is true but it is the idea of being left behind in the grim street, noticeably foreign and burdened with equipment that finally convinces me to make the short climb. The rubble has filled in the space between 6 or 8 blocks, which stand empty. I imagine the rubble shifting, losing my footing and airlocks.

John and Yan are already ahead of me. I am finding my feet. Finding that the rubble under foot is compacted and stable. Of course the residents of Xiancun use this route everyday. One of them is walking towards me now, along the rubble track towards a washing line strung between two derelict buildings. He avoids my gaze and the thinness of my smile that never got going. He adds the upholstery from a baby car seat to the line of personal belongings already hanging there. On my left rubble stops at the edge of a room. There is a row of pink fluffy slippers with cartoon faces, which I have to read as a poignant symbol, a clear and deliberate statement against the demolition of these homes. Deeper into the room, behind the slippers, I can see a woman's face, a reproduction of a painted portrait that has apparently come off the wall, landing askew. Apart from this still life the room is a concrete shell. This is a scene awaiting the photographer, an image stalking the lens. A media ready-made created by a village activist? A resident's memorial to a former life? Or maybe a still life constructed by a previous photographer?

The height of the rubble, over 10 metres maybe, means that we are on the same level as 2nd or 3rd floor windows. Some of the window apertures are filled with precarious and attractive arrangements of stacked bricks, others are open, the window glass is long gone. Yan climbs into one of the flats, to see if we can access the higher floors. He returns, shaking his head. There is no staircase.

The most tangible evidence of the remaining population in the urban village is the washing hanging out to dry. How to dry the washing appears to be the perennial problem of everyday life in Guangzhou and the urban village is no exception. Since very few people have tumble driers here and most live in apartments they have to negotiate the problem of how to dry the washing. Balconies are festooned with clothes hanging from racks, 4 or 5 rows deep. High levels of humidity and lack of air flow in the balconies, building recesses, hallways and lobbies where washing hangs, means that the task of drying is endless and dominates the domestic landscape. In the urban village demolition has created new opportunities for drying clothes. Lines have been strung between empty flats across the mounds of rubble. Clothes hang along fences and in window cavities where sometimes a shirt hanging out to dry can be mistaken for a figure. The lines of coloured washing add personality to the endless grey-white of the concrete rubble and the remaining holding hands houses that replaced the traditional village homes.

We are occupying a small rubble hillock with tripods and cameras. However critical we might wish it to be, the photographic process as it stands-making images to show others how things look when they look most like themselves, or alternatively most extraordinary-inevitably involves stalking moments. On the steep mound of rubble above where the man with the cropped hair sits by the lake, we are about to photograph an abandoned settee. At this moment a woman arrives, places straw beach mats over the settee and precedes to lay her washing under the sun. We do not photograph her as she goes about her domestic chores in public. Not all photographs can, nor should be taken.

Alongside the soft, everyday signifiers provided by washing on lines, we note the more trenchant symbols: the red flags flying atop of buildings. Yan tells us that the red flags indicate the dwellings of residents determined to remain. Waiting for John at the side of the road, I am talking to Yan about these villagers who stay on, the ones presiding over future nail houses. He

says that some of them are trying to get the most money they can and not everyone has sympathy for that. He asks me what I think, what do I really think about the situation? I tell him that I don't think it matters so much about individual motives. What if some people are motivated by money? It doesn't change the fact that as a whole this area has been decimated because of corporate interest. This is a global problem and it is always the poor who are forced to leave their homes and sometimes this is achieved through violence. Yan seems satisfied with this response and he tells me that a few years ago he witnessed a protest against the evictions, which lasted for several days, during which time many villagers were badly beaten by the police.

Yan keeps looking at his phone. He is using a fluctuating GPS to navigate through the narrow streets. I imagine us, tiny figures waving to the unseeing eye of a satellite. Before long we find ourselves at the edge of the village. Leaving as the migrant workers are returning from their work on the East tower or one of the other high-rise buildings in the business district,

to have lunch in the urban village. We pass a group of them in the elegant underpass, which opens into a wide circle of sky around which the towers of offices, hotel and board rooms peek. Through the brown film of pollution, which covers the Google earth image, Xiancun is almost a perfect square edged by tree-lined roads. The flat roofs of the village look like an industrial zone. To the west of Xiancun is a pendant shaped area of parkland rimmed with towers, this is the "diamond necklace" of Landmark Plaza's, which culminates in the jewel of Haixinsha Island, decked out for the 2010 Asian Games. The somewhat more prosaic Regus tower, which has offices to rent per day, leans towards the urban village, casting in its wake a shadow in the form of a lozenge. The Google earth satellite image, taken in 2015, clearly shows the demolition at the interior of the village. From the air the rubble mounds we scaled earlier look like a single rough-hewn track, carelessly scooped out from the dense housing. Viewed from the air the small lake fringed with washing lines is like a mouth open, aghast.

Kevin Crooks

INTERVIEWED
BY BRIAN J MORRISON

Brian J Morrison
is an artist and lecturer in Photography
at the University of Central Lancashire

Kevin Crooks
is a St. Helens based photographer
who has recently won the Deutsche
Bank Award for Creative Enterprise
after completing an MA in Photography
at the University of Central Lancashire.
Since completing his undergraduate
education Kevin has worked profession-
ally within the field of photography,
producing a range of projects that tackle
social and spatial mobility and the
politics of community. Kevin is currently
Head of Photography at Carmel College.

BRIAN J MORRISON: I would like to begin with your most recent work, M62 Scammonden which incorporates, photography, video, oral histories and archival material, can you give me a description of the project and the key themes as you see them?

KEVIN CROOKS: The project initially stemmed from an assignment that I completed as part my MA at UCLan. The Module called 'Space, Location and Territory', allowed me to choose a location and landscape that interested me and to produce a project in response.

I had always been intrigued by the M62 motorway and its surrounding landscape, and was initially drawn to this location as I thought that the environment would be challenging to document but yet visually interesting.

My preparatory studies consisted of researching material which commented upon the concept, motives, design and construction of the motorway. I have recently been working on a project which documented the closure of the North West Sound Archive, and following a discussion that I had with the sound archivist who worked there, he recommended that I listen to an oral history recording which consisted of an interview conducted with a construction worker, Stewart Bradbury who had worked on the building of the M62 motorway between junction 21 at Milnrow and Junction 24, Huddersfield/Halifax. Stewart talked of the role that he had and the details of the contract and what was involved in his day-to-day work. However, he also commented upon the impact the construction had, not only on the workers but also those that were living within the communities that the motorway crossed through. He also mentioned a number of folkloric tales, along with the story of the circumstances of the farmer at Stott Hall farm, where the farmhouse is sandwiched between both carriageways.

Although I was interested in the impact the motorway had brought to those people who were directly involved with the construction of the motorway, I was however more focussed, at this stage on demonstrating how the industrialisation of the landscape, particularly through the inclusion of the motorway, had irreversibly altered and manipulated the environment in which it was situated. This was in direct response to an assignment brief that was delivered as part of the Space, Location & Territory module, titled 'The Anthropocene City'

My original intention was to document one space, which would allow me the possibility of examining information on a more global scale, in the hope that I could provide some comprehensive and contemplative images that would provoke and provide a visual explanation of the Anthropocene and its effects. I began to think of spaces, environments and landscapes that have witnessed clear and dramatic man-made changes over a prolonged period of time. The M62 has developed, altered and has been manipulated into the motorway it is today because of its ever-increasing need to accommodate an ever-growing population. The environment in which the entire length of the motorway is situated will continue to change through the need and desire for it to be more economically efficient, provide more economic growth, allow for sustainable development and be more environmentally considerate.

These thoughts and considerations which were initiated in response to the research conducted throughout my MA studies, then allowed me to consider what is the 'M62' today, and how will the future developments of the motorway affect the regions that it travels through? In a climate of economic austerity, can the M62 contribute to the suggested necessity towards the creation and sustainability of a Northern Powerhouse?

I see the motorway as a visual reference; there is a contradiction within the motorway, it is there to connect people and places, however the people who travel on the motorway are somewhat detached, not only from the landscape that they travel through but also the people, who occupy the same stretch of motorway within cars that travel the very same route that they themselves are travelling.

There is a specific focus on connectivity in George Osborne's vision of how the Northern Powerhouse is to be created and facilitated, however do the towns that the motorway passes through really benefit from these initiatives?

Have the towns (and cities) that the M62 travels through really benefitted from the inclusion of the motorway, in the same way that increased connectivity through the creation of the Northern Powerhouse is to be envisaged?

BJM: This notion of contradiction would appear to have a significant role in the visualisation of your research, specifically when we considered much of the recent criticism surrounding the specifics of Osborne's Northern Powerhouse vision. Has it been this aspect that has driven you to include oral histories from construction workers involved, alongside archive material and your own photography?

KC: Initially the inclusion of the oral histories within this project was to provide my potential audience with an adequate and appropriate insight into the development of the project. Although the research element of the project was conceptualised through the studies that I had conducted, in reference to the themes and content that I wished to visualise and communicate. I was, however adamant, and felt that it was important and useful, to adopt a practice-based research method and approach which could aid the continued development and refinement of the production of the project. Therefore, although I had clear objectives throughout the project in terms of the progress that I intended to make, I was also very determined to allow and encourage opportunities to arise, that would possibly enable me to pursue and consider other alternative contributions that could, and would often assist with facilitating and creating more concise, interesting, dynamic, in-depth outcomes.

During the conception of the project and the initial planning stages, I was clear that I wanted to respond to the challenge of photographing a motorway that has a number of negative connotations attached to it. Motorways are naturally often seen as ugly, man made necessities that are constructed without any consideration as to how they are situated within a landscape. This is in fact incorrect and became increasingly more apparent through the studies that I was conducting.

The M62 motorway and it's surrounding Pennine landscape, visually reflect the industrialisation of the north of England. Although the motorway is situated within a landscape that, in parts has remained untouched for many centuries, there are areas within this landscape that have witnessed significant and irreversible manipulations and alterations. All of which have been a result of increased populations within the towns and cities within the region, and the economic and infrastructural needs to support this growth.

George Osborne's vision was to rebalance the economy of the country by improving and realising existing and new infrastructure programmes which would be utilised to stimulate and sustain economic growth.

'Our shared aim is to transform Northern growth, rebalance the country's economy and establish the North as a global powerhouse.' (Department for Transport, 2015)

In light of the result of the EU referendum vote, it is difficult to see how George Osborne's vision is to be now realised within this current parliament. However the Government has recently appointed Andrew Percy as the new Northern Powerhouse Minister who has confirmed that 'I've been in post 10 days now but I wanted to make it clear that the Northern Powerhouse is here to stay' and has stated that 'It's about bridging that gap between northern and southern' economies (Murphy, 2016)

BJM: Indeed, there is a shroud of uncertaintaity around many societal and economic aspects of post Brexit, Britain, and perhaps most significantly the freedom of movement of people and produce. To come back to the visual material for a moment, for me it evokes an almost classical tragedy, with paradoxical components and potential responses. Is there an attempt here to poeticise an otherwise fairly unpoetic aspect of society?

KC: Throughout my research I was keen on depicting the motorway, which is usually seen as an unwanted feature of a landscape, in a way that allows for more considered appreciation of not just the motorway but also how it sits, sympathetically and appropriately within the overall context of the landscape. A motorway is a dominant feature within any landscape, however when travelling through and over the Pennines the M62 becomes a dramatic and dominant feature which sits within a number of expansive, vast and open vistas.

Motorists are provided with the opportunity to appreciate and consider a significant and historic section of the northern landscape, which is only possible through the inclusion of the motorway. By what other means would such a large quantity of the population be able to view this area and the vistas that it has to offer?

It would be easy to conclude that the motorway, particularly within the Pennine section is a scar that unsympathetically cuts through a natural and untouched landscape. However, this landscape had been manipulated, exploited and altered long before the inclusion of the motorway. This environment has witnessed significant and irreversible changes, particularly as a result of the significant industrialisation of the north throughout the Industrial Revolution. For example, the reservoirs and dams, which scatter this landscape, were created to provide water for rapidly growing populations, as well as feeding the canal system, whilst also providing the ever-growing number of factories and mills within the region with a reliable and plentiful water supply.

The weather and terrain within the Pennine area has historically restricted the accessibility of the landscape, and although the hills separate and divide this northern region, the communities, towns and cities have cultural commonalities, which have been present, and have developed over a number of centuries. The motorway and the other routes over the Pennines have provided easier mobility and connectivity, which has aided the growth and development of the communities that they connect. Therefore, is it not essential that we continue to manipulate and alter our landscape to facilitate the growth and development of the northern region? Or, should we consider more creative, sympathetic, appropriate and sustainable alternatives?

Bibliography
Murphy, L. (2016) *New minister
says northern powerhouse
'here to stay' during Liverpool visit.*
Available at: http://www.liver-
poolecho.co.uk/news/liverpool-news/
new-minister-says-northern-power-
house-11673177
(Accessed: 8 August 2016).

*The Northern Powerhouse: One Agenda,
One Economy, One North (2015)*

Available at: https://www.gov.uk/
government/uploads/system/
uploads/attachment_data/
file/427339/the-northern-power-
house-tagged.pdf
(Accessed: 8 August 2016).

Mirzoeff (2014) *'Visualizing
the Anthropocene'*, Public Culture,
26(2 73), pp. 213–232. doi:
10.1215/08992363-2392039.

School of Journalism and Media

DR ANDREW IRELAND
EXECUTIVE DEAN

JOHN HOLLOWAY
HEAD OF SCHOOL

ALAN KEEGAN
PROGRAMME LEADER

Photography Department

JOHN VAN AITKEN
BA & MA COURSE LEADER

DR GARY BRATCHFORD
SENIOR LECTURER

DAVID DENNISON
LECTURER

JOANNA GARRETT
TECHNICIAN

ADAM MEAD
LECTURER &
TECHNICAL DEMONSTRATOR

BRIAN J MORRISON
LECTURER

JONATHAN PURCELL
LECTURER

MARK REEVES
LECTURER

DAVID SCHOFIELD
SENIOR TECHNICIAN

DAN TIERNEY
LECTURER &
TECHNICAL DEMONSTRATOR

North

PROJECT MANAGER
BRIAN J MORRISON

DESIGNED BY
BEN MCLAUGHLIN

PRINTED BY
UNICUM/GIANOTTEN PRINTED MEDIA

WITH A SPECIAL THANKS TO THE
CONTINUED SUPPORT FROM THE UNIVERSITY
OF CENTRAL LANCASHIRE, PRESTON

PUBLISHED NOVEMBER 2016
ISBN 978-1-909755-08-6

First published 2016 by the University of
Central Lancashire, Preston, PR1 2HE.

Part of The Great Northern Creative Festival,
The Fieldworks Conference and the Photography
Research Group.

WWW.UCLAN.AC.UK
WWW.PHOTOUCLAN.COM

University of Central Lancashire